Text by
**VITTORIO ROSSI**

# VICENZA
## historical-artistical itineraries
78 colour photographs and six itinerary maps

GINO ROSSATO PUBLICATION

# INDEX

## Itinerary n. 1 p. 11

Campo Marzo - Giardino Salvi: the two lodges - Torrione di Porta Castello - Palazzo Bonin Longare - Chiesa dei Filippini - Palazzo Loschi-Zileri - La Cattedrale (Duomo) - Loggetta Zeno in Vescovado - Il Criptoportico romano - Tempio di S. Lorenzo (2) - Palazzo Valmarana-Braga (1) - Palazzo Repeta - Palazzo Cordellina - Biblioteca Bertolina and Palazzo Costantini - Chiesetta SS. Giacomo and Filippo - Palazzo Trissino.


## Itinerary n. 2 p. 25

Palazzo Barbaran da Porto in Contrà Porti - Palazzo Thiene now Banca Popolare Vicentina in Contrà Porti - Palazzo Porto-Breganze Cattolica Assicurazione, in Contrà Porti - Palazzo Porto-Colleoni now - Palazzo Iseppo da Porto now Festa in Contrà Porti - Monte di Pietà in Contrà del and Piazza dei Signori - Chiesa di S. Vincenzo in Piazza dei Signori - La Basilica in Piazza dei Signori - La Loggia Bernarda in Piazza dei Signori - Palazzo da Schio in Corso - Palazzo Thiene now Banca Popolare Vicentina in Contrà S. Gaetano - Palazzo Sesso-Zen now Fontana in Piazzetta S. Stefano - Chiesa di S. Stefano in Piazzetta S. Stefano - Palazzo Leoni-Montanari now Banca Cattolica del Veneto in Contrà S. Corona - Chiesa di S. Corona in Contrà S. Corona - Casa Cogollo in Corso - Palazzo del Territorio and Teatro Olimpico in Piazza Matteotti - Palazzo Chiericati now Museo Civico in Piazza Matteotti.


## Itinerary n. 3 p. 47

Le Barche in Contrà Barche and Vicolo Cieco Retrone - Ponte S. Michele - Oratorio di S. Nicola, Piazzetta S. Nicola - Palazzo Valle, Contrà Busa S. Michele - Palazzo Gualdo, Piazza Gualdi - Palazzo Porto Scaroni (Teatro Berga) in front of Porton del Luzzo - Porton del Luzzo - Oratorio di S. Chiara in Contrà S. Chiara - Chiesa di S. Caterina in Contrà S. Caterina - Oratorio delle Zitelle in Contrà S. Caterina - Casa Pigafetta in Contrà Pigafetta - I Proti in Contrà Proti - Palazzi Arnaldi in Contrà Pasini - Chiesa delle Grazie in Piazzetta delle Grazie.


## Itinerary n. 4 p. 59

Basilica di S. Felice in Corso San Felice - Badia di S. Agostino - La Rocchetta - Chiesa S. Maria Nova in Contrà S. Maria Nova - Chiesa di S. Rocco in Piazzetta S. Rocco - Chiesa dei Carmini in Piazzetta dei Carmini - Palazzo Volpe - Gallo - Zaccaria. The "Vigna" Foundation - Chiesa di S. Croce - Porta S. Croce.


## Itinerary n. 5 p. 69

Chiesa di S. Marco in Contrà S. Marco - Parco Querini, viale Bacchiglione - Chiesa dell'Araceli Piazza Araceli - Porta S. Lucia - Palazzo Magrè Angaran Piazza XX Settembre - Ponte degli Angeli - Corte dei Roda, Contrà S. Andrea - Chiesa di S. Pietro, Piazzetta S. Pietro - Oratorio dei Boccalotti - S. Domenico in Contrà Domenico.


## Itinerary n. 6 p. 79

Arco delle Scalette, Piazzale Fraccon - Villa Valmarana ai Nani, Piazzetta S. Bastiano - Villa Capra "La Rotonda", strada Valmarana - Basilica di Monte Berico - Piazzale della Vittoria - Villa Guiccioli and park (Risorgimento Museum), Viale X Giugno - Portici - Chiesetta di S. Giorgio in Viale Fusinato.

# Introduction

The beauty of Vicenza's buildings and monuments, together with the compact nature of its old centre make the writing of a brief guide at the same time easy and difficult.

Easy because of the wealth of information available, and difficult because of the range of cultural and artistic reference points and the number of simple platitudes and clichés which have been attached to them.

To get to know Vicenza, to reveal its secrets, the visitors has to carefully explore the town at first hand, otherwise it will reveal only its external appearance, and nothing if its soul.

The various eras which the town has gone through; Roman, Gothic, Baroque and Neoclassical have all left their mark, but to unravel this complicated past and understand the town's present requires some effort on the part of the visitor.

With these points in mind the guide has been laid out with the following two aims:

1 Avoid the over complications of a stuffy traditional guide, which may put the visitor off right from the beginning.
2 Bring out, through the walks described in the guide, the historical development of the town, without bringing in unnecessary or confusing information.

For these reasons we have chosen to start our visit from the outskirts of the town, rather than the central Piazza Matteotti, so we may bring back to life, through the buildings and monuments, the historical development of the town, from its Paleoveneto origins to the present day.

# The topography of the town

Vicenza is situated at the foot of the south side of the Monte Berici, and is built on an area of gently rolling land produced by the irregular flooding of the Astico and Retrone rivers. Today two rivers flow into the town, joining in the middle (the Bacchiglione and the Retrone), but the modern day layout of the rivers and streams reflects only in part that found in the past. Only the Retrone held its course through the centuries, running more or less parallel to the Brenta south of Padua, reaching the sea near Chioggia, and once navigable for its entire length. Following the hydrographic changes made in the Veneto during the Lombardic era, which generally redirected the rivers towards the north-east, the Brenta, which during the Roman times flowed through the town, began to run to the west of Padua. The Bacchiglione on the other hand, is a more recent river which has its origins in the gravel beds of the River Astico, and which in Roman times followed almost the same course as the Astichello, but blocked by its sedimentary deposits just outside the town formed a lake known as "Pusteria". From here it flowed on to the north-west of the present day Viale Rodolfi and beyond Araceli ran between St. Corona and St. Pietro, joining the Retrone downstream from Isola (now Piazza Matteotti). Isola was thus named because it was surrounded by water, as from Canove there was a stream, the Collo, which flowed into the Retrone near the Barche bridge. The rectangular layout of the town during Roman times, determined by the hydrographical situation, may still be seen today, between Piazza Duomo, north-east end of Corso Palladio, Pedemuro S. Biagio and the S. Paolo bridge. The town was criss-crossed by streets running at 90° to each other forming large blocks. The town was crossed by the Via Postumi, which went from Genoa to Aquileia and ran through Vicenza along the "decumanus maximus". During this period the town saw considerable development of its population and economy, whereas following the fall of the Roman Empire in 476 A.D. there was a slowing down of its growth, if not a decline. To protect themselves from invasion the people of Vicenza built an elliptical wall around the town, and the artificial banks on which the walls were built, called "Mottoni", gave their names to the oldest streets in the town: Motton S. Lorenzo, Motton S. Corona, Motton Pusteria.

The walls limited space, and the streets of the town were thus narrow and winding. Building of the "borghi" took place outside the wall, including Portanuova S. Pietro and S. Caterina and Borgo Berga. Borgo Berga, settled by the Lombards, expanded greatly towards the "Riviera", and the city walls came to need extending.

This extension was begun by the Scaligeri, during the second half of the 14th century, and enclosed Portanuova and S. Pietro within powerful new defenses. Under Venetian domination in the 16th century Vicenza underwent a great transformation from medioeval town of gothic buildings to a town enriched by the work of the architect Andrea Palladio backed by ambitions noblemen, the results of whose combined forces were to be come famous all over the world.

The real growth in population however took place during the 19th and early 20th century, the period which coincides with the arrival of the first major industries: the railways and brickworks. Another substantial increase in urban development took place after the second World War and in 1965 Vicenza reached a population of 100,000.

New residential suburbs have sprung up around the town, particulary along the SS 11 road to the east and west, and along the Riviera Berica. These developments have swallowed a areas of agricultural land and the old term "borghi" and "colture" have been replaced by the modern "circoscrizione".

In addition to new residential areas Vicenza has important industrial estates, but as least as far as the tourist is concerned the old town centre remains of most interest.

## History

Man has lived around the Vicenza area since prehistoric times, as proven by archaelogicl finds including those around the Fimon lake. The first inhabitants were the Euganei who occupied a large area between the gulf of Monfalcone, the mouth of the Adige and the land to the south of lake Iseo, around two thousand years B.C.. Around the 8th C. the indoeuropean Veneti arrived from Illarise, pushing the Euganei to the higher ground where they took refuge in the Pre-alps. At the end of the Second Punic war, when Rome conquered Gallier Cisalpine and Illiria, the towns of the Veneto, including Vicenza, fell under Roman rule (177 B.C.). Thus began one of the most fortunate periods in the town's history. The agricultural economy was backed up by brickworks, marble was quarried in the nearby mountains and the first woollen industry developed. The religion was Roman and the cult of Diana was particularly well followed. Unprotected by defensive walls and situated right on the Via Postumia Vicenza was repeatedly sacked by Barbarian hordes which invaded Italy between the 4th and 5th centuries, and the rebuilding of the town was still unfinished when the Vandals and the Alani arrived in 464 A.D.

Following the fall of the Western Roman Empire in 476, the romanised Barbarian Odoacre came to the throne, and this wise ruler allowed his subjects to practise their Christian faith.

Next came the Lombards, who, following their invasion in 568 turned Vicenza into a duchy with its own currency. In 773 Carlo Magno came to Italy, called by Pope Adrian I, and Vicenza passed into the hands of the Franchi and became a county. The descendents of Carlo Magno however proved themselves unfit to rule, and a period of confusion, weakness and ignorance followed.

August of 899 saw the invasion of the much feared Hungarians, who captured the defenceless Vicenza, sacking and destroying the monastery of S. Felice.

The people of Vicenza thus decided to build a protective wall around the town, and look-out posts were put up on most houses. In the surrounding countryside castles were built by important landowners and bishops, with the aim of defending the population and their places of worship.

The crowning by the Pope of Ottone II of Germany in 962

signified the rebirth of the Sacred Roman Empire. In 983 Ottone III, in line with trends set by his predecessor, favoured the clergy by making castles belonging to the church exempt from the "fodro" tax.

Even during its darkest hours Vicenza had maintained its Roman traditions, and the power of the Lombard dukes and Frankish counts was limited to the city.

In the 9th and 10th centuries the counts' power was limited to the surrounding countryside, while the city itself was ruled by the bishops. The state of affairs lasted until the uprising against bishop Tarengo in 1110.

By 1115 Vicenza was a free town with magistrates, courts and town council. Great economic and social change took place and the middle classes because increasingly important at the expense of the feudatory nobility. Following more than seventy years of fighting and rivalry, particular with Padua and Ezzelino, Vicenza finally received the liberty of the city-states of Veneto, setting up its own city-state government.

The end of the 12th century however saw a re-opening of hostilities between Padua and Vicenza, which was now backed by Ezzelino. Eventually a delegation from Vicenza sued for peace and Padua effectively held the keys to the city for some 45 years, until Enrico VII of Luxemburg joined forces with Vicenza against Padua. Enrico gave the task of regaining the city to the bishop of Genevra, who was banked by Cangrande della Scala, and the following period saw a great deal of rebuilding and a resurgence of art and culture. However, Vicenza once again became involved in hostilities, this time with the Scaligeri against Padua, until power passed into the hands of Giangaleazzo Visconti in 1387. This unhappy reign lasted only twenty years, until in 1404 Gianpietro Proti and Giacomo Thiene gave the city to Venetian Republic. The republic decided that the city should continue to govern itself in accordance with existing statutes, with the exception that the rector had to be Venetian.

This period should be remembered for the imitation of Venetian architecture at the beginning of the century and that of Lombardy/Emilia towards and end, the development of printing and the establishment of a system of pawnbroking. From 1500 to 1700 Vicenza and its hard-working people enjoyed a period of stability and prosperity. Industries such as wood and silk spinning and weaving and ceramics boomed, while poets writers, artists and architects met, encouraged by willing followers. Thus we come to Andrea Palladio, whose works so enriched the area, giving a new look to the town and a new direction in architecture to the rest of Europe and the whole world.

This period of development was not without its negative episodes, such as the epidemics, which killed more citizens than all the wars. Victims were isolated in the "Ospedale di Nazareth" near the S. Giorgio church in Gogna. The single plague of 1630 killed over 11.000 people in Vicenza and 30.000 in the whole province.

The early 1700's saw the arrival of the spirit of liberty, equality and fraternity, which brought about first the American and then the French revolutions. Italian cities looked towards Napoleon, whose armies, after a brief hold-up in Verona reached the cities of the Veneto, including Vicenza on April 27th 1797. In the same year the treaty of Campoformio marked the end of the Republic of Venice and the exchange by France and Austria of the Veneto for Lombardy. The first Austrian occupation lasted until 1805. Vicenza then became part of the kingdom of Italy.

In 1812 Napoleon was heavily defeated in Russia, and in 1814 the victors met in Vienna. Vicenza was joined with the kingdom of Lombardy and Veneto which was handed to Austria in 1815. There then followed a period of economic decline, with trade and industry being hampered by political barriers.

The discontent ran through all social classes, and culminated in rebellion against the occupiers in 1848. On the 10th of June these was a fierce battle on Monte Berico. The city was subsequently beseiged by Radetzky and the rebels were forced to capitulate in order to save the town.

Liberation finally came in 1866, after the third war of independence, when Italian troups freed the Veneto from Austrian rule.

Peace then reigned until 1815, when there was fierce fighting on Monte Pasubio, the Altopiano dei Sette Comuni and Monte Grappa. The second World War on the other hand saw many Vicenza men die on distant fronts and in concentration camps, whilst in Vicenza itself bombing killed many and destroyed much.

Following the end of the second World War the people of Vicenza began the rebuilding of their town, and thus we arrive at the town as we find it today.

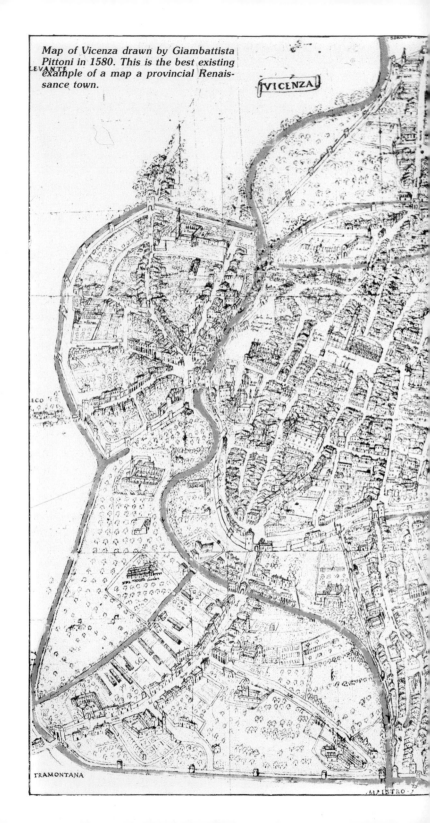

Map of Vicenza drawn by Giambattista Pittoni in 1580. This is the best existing example of a map a provincial Renaissance town.

VICENZA

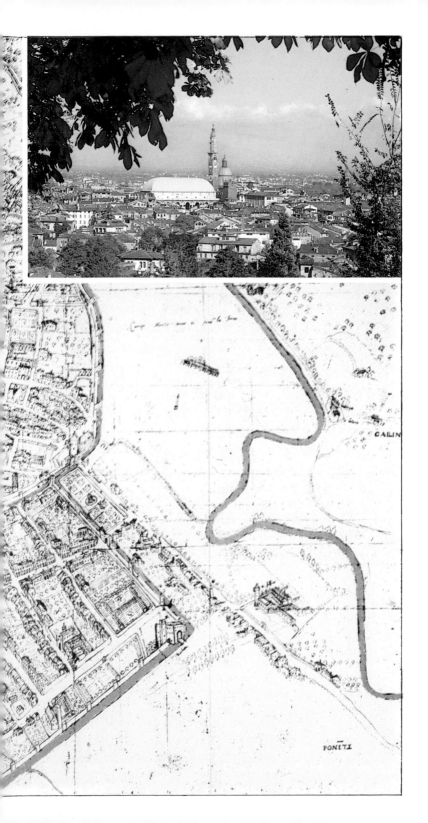

*View of the Palladio Basilica, reflected in the river Retrone*

# ITINERARY N. 1
## On foot. Time required: 3 hours

*Focal points:*

1) Campo Marzo
2) Giardino Salvi: the two lodges
3) Torrione di Porta Castello
4) Palazzo Bonin Longare
5) Chiese dei Filippini
6) Palazzo Loschi-Zileri
7) La Cattedrale (Duomo)
8) Loggetta Zeno in Vescovado
9) Il Criptoportico romano
10) Tempio di S. Lorenzo
11) Palazzo Valmarana-Braga
12) Palazzo Repeta
13) Palazzo Cordellina
14) Biblioteca Bertoliana and Palazzo Costantini
15) Chiesetta SS. Giacomo and Filippo
16) Palazzo Trissino

## The Route:

Viale Roma - Piazzale De Gasperi - Giardino Salvi - Piazza Castello - Corso Palladio - Stradella Loschi - Piazza Duomo - Via Cesare Battisti - Corso Fogazzaro - Contrà Riale - Stradella S. Giacomo - Piazzetta S. Giacomo - Corso Palladio.

Going along Viale Roma, away from the station we see Campo Marzo, the largest and oldest of Vicenza's public parks. The name 'Marzo' comes from 'marcita' meaning a marshy place with stagnant water. Continuing along Viale Roma, past Viale Dalmazia on our right we come to the square in which until 1938 stood an arch of triumph, built in 1608 by order of Pier Paolo Battaglia, Captain of Venice.

At the end of Viale Roma we find the entrance arch to the Giardino Salvi. The park was first laid out in 1552 by Count Giacomo di Valmarana, modified in 1826 and extended in 1845.

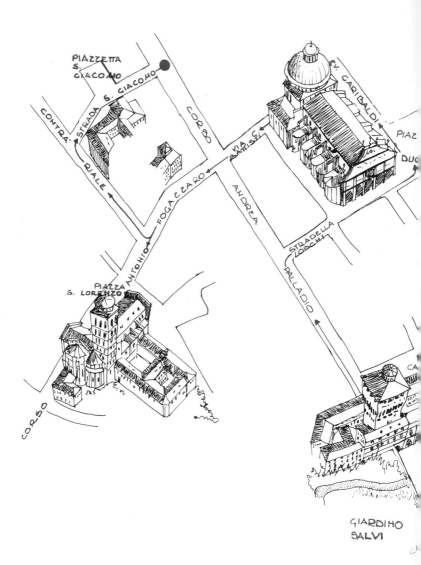

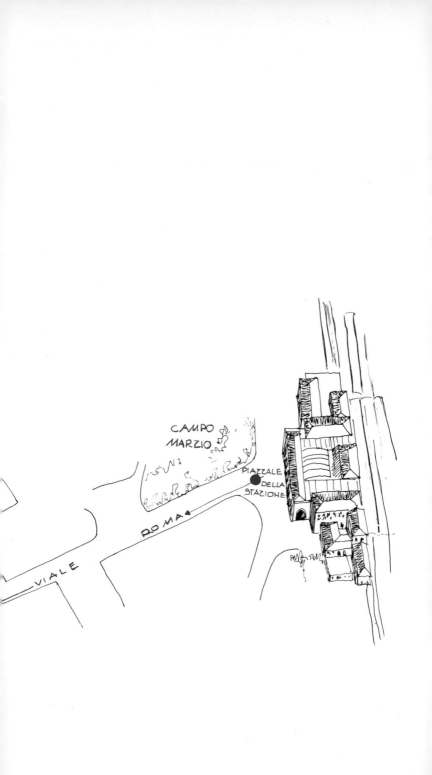

CAMPO
MARZIO

PIAZZALE
DELLA
STAZIONE

ROMA

VIALE

*Salvi gardens arch and the Torrione di Porta Castello*

Open to the public since 1907 the park is bound on two sides by the Seriola stream, and has two beautiful lodges. The first, by Palladio is built on the stream, while the second by Longhena is in the west corner. From the entrance to the park we have a fine view of the Torrione di Porta Castella.

The main body of the tower dates back to 1200, and battlements and the interesting hexagonal lanterns were added in 1343 by Bernardo Scannabecchi following instructions by Martino and Alberto della Scala. Passing the tower we find the 17th C. entrance to the courtyard of Palazzo Salvi to our left and the impressive spacious Piazza Castello on our right. On the far side of the square, to the right we see the unfinished Palazzo Porto-Breganze, attributed to Palladio, whilst on our left is Palazzo Piovini, now Corsi, built in 1658 by Antonio Pizocaro. Facing Palazzo Piovini on Corso Palladio we have the majestic Palazzo Bonin Longare. Whilst the building bears certain hallmarks of the Palladian style the outline of the facade and the siting of the half columns do not indicate the hand of the maestro himself. The hall and the piano nobile, connected to the lodge are of better design.

Our walk continues along Corso Palladio. On the right after Palazzo Piovini we have the 17th C. facade of Palazzo Bissari, followed by the severe noble lines of Palazzo Braghetta Pagello, next to which we find the most important work of Ottone Calderari, Palazzo Loschi-Zileri Dal Verme, built in 1782. Opposite, on the site of the Chiesa del Gesù (1602-1718) is the Chiesa dei Filippini. The facade is an interpretation by Antonio Piovene of a design by Ottone Calderari, and was built in 1824. The inside, with the exception of a few modifications, is the work of Giorgis Massari. The altars are by Antonio Piovese.

Next to the church, along the stradella dei Filippini, is the Convento dei Padri Filippini, begun in 1801 by Giacomo Fontana, a pupil of Calderari. Connected to the convent is the oratorium by Carlo Fontano built between 1801 and 1803.

Continuing along stradella Loschi we come to the Duomo. The facade looks over a small square, preventing us from get-

*The cathedral (Duomo)*

ting a better view. Dedicated to Santa Maria Maggiore, the Duomo is a powerfully-built Gothic cathedral which is built over other churches, and has undergone various modifications. About two and a half metres below the Duomo lie the remains of an 8th C. basilica and another, with no less than five naves, dating from the 11th. Just twenty centimetres under the present floor are the foundations of yet another basilica, with three naves, probably dating from the 13th C. It seems certain that on this site a sacred building existed during the Roman rule of the paleo-Christian era.

The facade dates back to 1467, as shown on the upper frieze, and is covered by pink and white marble in four horizontal bands. The lower part has five large arches, with the middle one containing the main door, the surround of which was built in 1782 by Calderari. The second band is divided into five parts by pilaster strips, with a central rose window, the third is free of detail, whilst the fourth, built in 1950, replaces the pedi-

*Palazzo Bonin-Longare now Ass. Industriali*

*Loggia Valmarana in the Salvi gardens*

ment destroyed by a hurricane in 1581. Inside we find a large nave and seven chapels to right and left. The crypt is reached via stairs in front of the seventh chapel.

The choir, at the top of a large stairway, was designed by Lorenzo da Bologna (late 1400's) and built by Rocca da Vicenza (1506-1508). The valuable altar was commissioned from Giovanni de Pedemuro and Girolamo Pittoni by Aurelio Dall'Acqua in 1534. Work began slowly, but was then speeded up as it was believed the Anti-reformist Council would meet in Vicenza in 1539. In the end Pope Paolo III moved the meetings to Trento.

Leaving by the side door we find ourselves in Piazza del Duomo, with its central statue of Vittorio Emanuele II by Benvenuti (1880). The north side is taken up by the restored southern flank of the Duomo, whilst on the west side is the bishop's palace, which has undergone many changes since the late medioeval period. After asking for permission to enter the countyard we can admire the Zeno lodge, named after Cardinal Giambattista Zeno, and built by Bernardino da Milano (1494-95). Leaving the bishop's residence we continue to the right where we find the words 'Criptoportico romano' above a door. This crypt was discovered in 1954, and has been the subject of three excavations. It is situated under Palazzetto Proti and the Canonice next to it, three metres below the present level of the square. U-shaped, it has a total length of 83 metres, is 3.40 metres wide and between 2 metres and 2.80 metres high. Where the two side corridors meet the central one there are two interconnecting rooms with well-preserved doorways. The left-hand room is also connected to a sloping corridor which carried waste water to the Roman canal on the other side of the bishop's garden.

The walls are plastered, whilst the flooring is generally missing except for a few pieces of hexagonal mosaic, terracotta tiles or small tesseras.

Going back out into the square we continue past Palazzetto Proti (rebuilt following the last war) to the Oratorio del Gonfalone, built by the Confraternita del Gonfalone in 1596. Here too bombing took its toll and of the original interior only the main altar remains. Continuing towards Contrà Garibaldi we find the Torre Campanaria, the base of which is compased of large blocks of trachyte from the late Roman era, to which Dondi Dall'Orologio added a wood frame design.

*Tempio di S. Lorenzo*

*Palazzo Repeta now Banca d'Italia*

Continuing along Via Cesare Battisti, crossing Corso Palladio we go down Corso Fogazzaro. On the right we have the impressive Palazzo Valmarana-Brega Rosa, started in 1566 by Palladio but finished only in 1680. Palladio designed a building to stand on an irregularly shaped piece of ground running parallel with Corso Palladio and Contrà Reale, which could only be seen from close up. For this reason in the place of columns he used pilaster strips, which given the height of the facade, had to be of a great size. Beyond the entrance hall is the courtyard with two lodges. As often the case with Palladio's works this part remained unfinished. Next door we find Palazzo Valmarana-Rosi, of the same period, the soft Berici stone mouldings of which have been recently restored. On the left facing the entrance to Contrà Reale we find the rebuilt Palazzo Caldogno Tecchio, destroyed by bombing in January 1945.

*Palazzo Valmarana-Braga*

Opposite is Casa Piccioli, a Romanesque building which still
has a three-light window rebuilt during the Gothic period.
Reaching Piazza S. Lorenzo we see the facing Chiesa di S.

*Palazzo Costantini now Biblioteca Bertoliana*

Lorenzo and Palazzo Repeta. In the middle is a statue of Giacomo Zanella, a noted local poet.

Palazzo Repeta-Sale is one of the early works of Francesco Muttoni (1711). The church opposite, originally built in 1288, was closed following the Napoleonic invasion and was reopened for worship in 1839 after initial restoration. Further restoration took place between 1870 and 1927. The lower part of the facade comprises eight walled arches dating back to the 1300's, whilst the upper part is crowned by small blind arches and a rose window. The large central door has a sculpture of the Madonna and Child above it. Inside three long naves, finishing with the apse, have two lines of huge stone columns. In

*Palazzo Trissino, now Municipio*

the right hand part of the transept is the beautiful Pojana altar with its well-preserved triptych dating back to 1400. In the right hand wall are the remains of the poet Zanella. The presbytery contains two funeral monuments of the Da Porto family and two large paintings by Pittoni. In the chapel on the left, on an altar dating back to the 1700's we find a beautiful sculpture by Antonino da Venezia, showing the Madonna, Infant Jesus, Saint Peter and Saint Paul. At the end on the left is the Sagrestia leading to the 15th C. cloister.

Leaving the church by the side door we follow a piece of Roman road and then turn into Contrà Reale, which joins Corso Fogazzaro and Contrà Proti. After the two houses Loschi and Caldogno we come to Palazzo Cordellina on the left, a typical example of Vicenza neoclassicism designed by Calderari, who gave the plans as a gift to the nobleman Carlo Cordellina. The central part was damaged during World War Two, with the resulting loss of the frescoes in the central hall.

Opposite a small area of grass connects Palazzo Costantini with the ancient convent of S. Giacomo, now the town library, which holds valuable manuscripts from the 16th to 19th centuries. The library dates back to the 1700's.

Opposite the end of Stradella S. Giacomo we find the beautiful 14th C. portal of Palazzo Trissino-Lanza. Going down the Stradella we come to Chiesa SS. Filippo and Giacomo in Piazzetta S. Giacomo. Between 1583, when the Somaschi Fathers ran the parish and 1772 when they were expelled from Vicenza the church was radically transformed and the convent built. The Fathers, who arrived in Vicenza in 1558 were first unofficially and then ufficially responsible for the teaching and organization of the Seminary and the running of the orphanage of Maria della Misericordia, and in 1658 they also took over the hospital of S. Valentino alle Barche. The problems of the parish church were not only religious: the church was in need of restoration, and the living space available to the fathers was small. Thus, in 1588, began the request for alms money on the part of those involved in the church in Vicenza.

Up to 1600 the church was laid out opposite to its present day plan. The rebuilding, which took place in one year, 1602, was carried out according to designs by Monsignor Giovanni Giacomo Montecchio. In 1627 the church underwent further reconstruction following grave damage caused by the Veneto prohibition (1606-1607). The five chapels, the pendetives and

*Roman crypt*

the attic are richly decorated, with paintings by Maffei, Maganza and Carpioni. On the floor we may admire the beautiful terracotta tomb covers.

Leaving the church we pass under an arch and come back onto Corso Palladio. Almost opposite is the majestic Palazzo Trissino Baston, designed by Vincenzo Scamozzi for count Galeazzo Trissino in 1592. It was completed in 1662 by Antonio Pizzocaro and further extended by Calderari during the Neoclassic period. The Porto family gave the building to the town council in 1901. The building was badly damaged by fire on March 18th 1945, and many valuable paintings by Dorigny and all the stuccoes by Pizzocaro were destroyed. The right hand room facing Corso Palladio still has many pieces of the recently restored fresco by Carpioni.

## ITINERARY N. 2
## On foot. Time required: 3 hours

*Focal Points:*

1) Palazzo Barbaran da Porto in Contrà Porti
2) Palazzo Thiene now Banca Popolare Vicentina in Contrà Porti
3) Palazzo Porto-Breganze now Cattolica Assicurazione, in Contrà Porti
4) Palazzo Porto-Colleoni now R.A.S. in Contrà Porti
5) Palazzo Iseppo da Porto now Festa in Contrà Porti
6) Monte di Pietà in Contrà Del Monte and Piazza dei Signori
7) Chiesa di S. Vincenzo in Piazza dei Signori
8) La "Basilica" in Piazza dei Signori
9) La Loggia Bernarda in Piazza dei Signori
10) Palazzo da Schio in Corso
11) Palazzo Thiene now Banca Popolare di Vicenza in Contrà San Gaetano
12) Palazzo Sesso-Zen now Fontana in Piazzetta S. Stefano
13) Chiesa di S. Stefano in Piazzetta S. Stefano
14) Palazzo Leoni-Montanari now Banca Cattolica Del Veneto in Contrà S. Corona
15) Chiesa di S. Corona in Contrà S. Corona
16) Casa Cogollo in Corso
17) Palazzo del Territorio and Teatro Olimpico in Piazza Matteotti
18) Palazzo Chiericati now Museo Civico in Piazza Matteotti

## The Route:

From Corso Palladio - Contrà Porti - Contrà Del Monte - Piazza dei Signori - Piazza Biade - Contrà Del Monte - Via San Gaetano - Piazzetta Santo Stefano - Stradella Santo Stefano - Contrà Santa Corona - Corso - Piazza Matteotti or Isola.

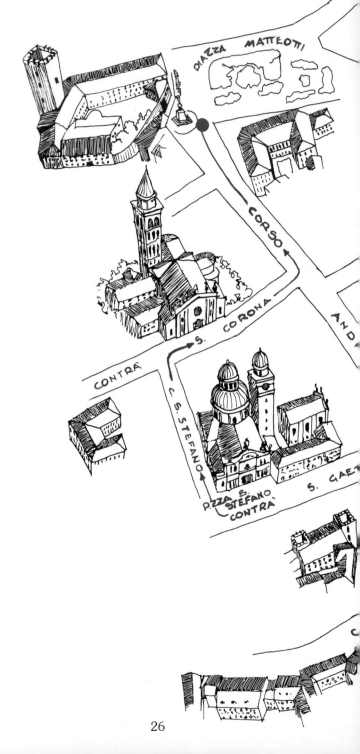

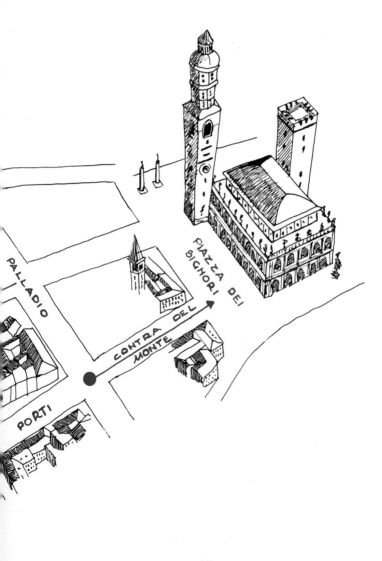

PALLADIO

PORTI

CONTRA DEL MONTE DEI

PIAZZA DEI SIGNORI

From Corso Palladio we go left into Contrà Porti, which is particularly rich in architectural content. The street takes its name from the numerous houses owned by the noble Porto family.

The building on the corner is the 16th C. Palazzo Breganze, and opposite is the early 15th C. Venetian-Gothic Palazzo di Thiene, which has undergone disastrous restoration. On the right we next come to Palazzo Thiene. The beautiful flowered doorway is attributed to Tommaso da Milano. Restorations carried out by Malacarne in 1872 have altered the facade, making the spacing of the windows symmetrical.

In 1542 Marcantonio Thiene decided to expand his family residence, built in Contrà Porti by Lorenzo da Bologna in 1489. The new palace designed by Andrea Palladio was to form a quadrilateral along the Contrà S. Gaetano Thiene and the Corso, joined at Contrà Porti. When the client died in 1560, this palace was left incomplete. The Banca Popolare di Vicenza bought it in 1872, making it its historical headquarters. The Palace has been restored to its former magnificence thanks to the recent, attentive restoration of the exterior and, most importantly, the interiors, where the frescoes, stucco decorations, ceilings and grotesques have been recovered. The visitors may therefore admire a sequence of rooms starting with the Palladiano Salon, the Hall of Grotesques, the Halls of Myths, Metamorphoses, Neptune, Persephone, the Princes and Psyche, and finally

*Palazzo Thiene now*
*Banca Popolare di Vicenza*

*Palazzo Porto Breganze now Assicurazione Cattolica Veronese*

the Hall of the Gods. The vaults with stucco finish and the sculptural decorations are by Alessandro Vittoria and Bartolomeo Ridolfi, while the paintings and the frescos are by Eliodoro Forbicini and Anselmo Canera.  Opposite is Palazzo Barbaran-Porto by Andrea Palladio, whose original plans for count Montano Barbarano were different from those finally used; statues were removed, bas-reliefs were built into the piano nobile windows and decorations were added. The symmetry of the building was also altered following the purchase of the building next door on the part of Count Barbarano. The best aspect of the building is the hall.

Moving on past Contrà Reale we come to three buildings of outstanding architectural merit. The first is Palazzo Porto-Breganze, now carefully restored by its present occupiers following damage during the last war and a period of falling into

*Palazzo Porto Colleoni*

general disrepair. It is a typical Gothic building with a quadrifora window with inverted arches. The doorway has a floral motif, and was designed by Lorenzo da Bologna.

The second of the three buildings is the Venetian-Gothic Palazzo Porto-Colleani. The facade has a quadrifora window. Beyond the main doors is the atrium with a Gothic staircase leading to the piano nobile. The courtyard was the site of a wooden theatre, typical of the first half of the 16th C., commissioned by a group of local gentlemen and designed by Sebastiano Serlio in 1539.

The third building is Palazzo Iseppo da Porto, now Festa.

This Palladian building, built between 1540 and 1549 was to have had two parts, one facing Contrà Porti and the other, which was never built, facing S. Biagio.

Going down Contrà Porti back to Corso Palladio we now go down Contrà del Monte to Piazza dei Signori. On the left we have the original home of the Biblioteca Bertoliana which held the books donated to the town by the juriconsult Giovanni Maria Bertolo. The building was commissioned by Marquis Scipione Repeta. the architect was Francesco Muttoni, and the whole building was built in one year starting from March 1704.

The Monte della Pietà dates back to 1409, and parts have been added down the ages since then, with the Loggia della Chiesa di S. Vincenzo being built in the middle of the building around 1615. Behind the lodge is the church, built in 1387, with its altar, as was then the practice, facing east. The church is composed of three parts; the first, inside the main door dating back to the 1300's, the second, the altar of the Pietà by Orazio Mainardi from the 1500's, and the third, the main altar by Muttoni, from the 1700's.

Going back out into the square we see on our left two columns in marble from the nearby valley of Chiampo. The placing of two columns on the shorter side of the square was a Veneto tradition, and these columns are topped by the lion

*Facade of the Chiesa di S. Vincenzo with the Monte della Pietà*

*Panoramic view of Vicenza with the Basilica by Palladio*

of Saint Mark and the figure of the redeemer. Beyond the columns is the part of the square which in medioeval times was used as a cereal market.

We now come to the most important building here, the Basilica, the first major work by Palladio and now the symbol of Vicenza. The contract to build the "loggia", the exterior part of the Basilica, was won by Palladio in competition with distinguished architects of the time, and his plans were not only to support the existing 15th C. unstable Gothic building inside his elegant but strongly built Basilica, but also to include the "Domus comestabilis". This did not happen however, and the building can still be seen next to the Torrione del Tormento, one of the few examples of medioeval Vicenza. "Basilica" as defined by Palladio himself means a court as known in Roman times, and the influence his visits to Rome had on the young architect are obvious in the regular arches and spaces so reminiscent of the Colosseum. Each arch is supported by a massive square pillar flanked by two semi-columns and two further small columns. The two series of 'loggia' go right round the dome and have narrow balconies.

The dome itself is in the shape of an upturned ship's hull, and is of copper sheeting over wooden supports, and the balustrade is decorated with statues of mythological figures.

The building was finished in 1617, thirty seven years after the death of Palladio.

*Piazza dei Signori*

*Loggia Bernarda or del Capitanio and Grancaffè Garibaldi*

Two stairways take us up to the Logge. One, facing Piazza delle Erbe, was built by Benatello around the end of the 16th C., whilst the other, facing Piazza dei Signori, is by da Milano.

This second Gothic staircase leads to the Salone, where we may admire the heavy beams supported by carved lion heads and emblems of the town. On the east wall is the "Leone di S. Marco". This room was used as a court and council chamber.

*… Basilica and Loggia del Capitanio*

From the Duomo Comestabilis we may go up to the upper terrace of the Basilica, from where there is an excellent view of the city and the Monte Berico.

On the left of the Basilica is the Torre di Piazza, 82 metres high and 7 m wide at the base. It was bought by the Bissari in

35

*Torre del Tormento with view of the Basilica*

1226, the belfry was opened in 1311, and the top was added in 1444. At the bottom in a large niche flanked by two columns is a stone carving of the Madonna on the throne, with Saint Vincent and Saint Stephen (1596). A passageway under the Basilica leads to the courtyard of Palazzo Podestarile.

Coming back into the square, looking to the left of Contrà del Monte we see Palladio's Loggia Bernardo, now the home of the town council. Started in 1571 the building has just three arches supported by strongly built pillars in unfaced brick, a clear sign of the master at work, whereas other fancier parts of the building, the stonework and balustrades for example, point to the fact that during construction Palladio was away in Venice. The side of the building nearest Contrà del Monte has a single arch and statues, as well as a stucco showing the victory of the Venetian fleet over the Turks in the battle of Lepanto (1571).

The upper room of the loggia once held paintings by Fasolo but now has frescoes taken from Villa Porto in Torre di Quartesolo.

Leaving the square by Contrà del Monte we come back to Corso Palladio, and on our right, just after Via S. Gaetano we come to the magnificent Gothic Cà d'oro. Built around 1400 it was almost completely destroyed by bombing during 1944, and was rebuilt in 1950. The building has a double row of balustrades, quadrifore windows and is delightfully symmetrical. The doorway by Lorenzo da Bologna is Rennaissance in style. Up to the last century the facade was covered by frescoes on a gold background. The courtyard has a number of stone tablets and Roman inscriptions collected last century by Conte Giovanni Da Schio.

Going back along Contrà S. Gaetano we find the solid presence of Palazzo Thiene, now a bank, on our left. This building was built between 1550 and 1558, and if Palladio's plans had been followed exactly would have today been one of the most imposing pieces of Italian architecture. It was to have taken

*Palazzo da Schio*

up an area between Contrà Porti, Contrà S. Gaetano, Stradella della Banca Popolare and Corso Palladio. Only an eighth was built, but this was sufficient to show the talents of the Maestro, who uses here for the first time the technique of rustification, learnt in Rome and Tuscany.

The inside of the building is impressive for its majesty and decoration. Walls and ceilings carry frescoes by Vittoria and del Ridolfi, and it is possible to go in to see the four statues showing Paris and other gods by Orazio Marinali.

Leaving the building we walk towards Piazzetta S. Stefano.

On the right we see the church of S. Stefano, until the 12th C. one of the seven chapels of Vicenza, and on the left the powerfully built palazzo Negri de Salvi, built around an earlier Roman construction.

Giving along Stradella S. Stefano we come to Contrà Santa Corona, full of buildings of architectural note. On the left, at the end of the street is Palazzo Leoni Montanari, now a bank, and which may be visited on Saturdays. The building of the Palazzo has a complex history, going back to 1776 when the Montanari family bought up a number of houses in the area belonging to silk-spinners. It took eleven years to complete the building and gave the inter-related Montanari and Leoni families the right to become noblemen and join the Council of the Five Hundred.

(visits: Friday, Saturday, Sunday) from: Palazzo Leoni Montanari. The building underwent a first radical reconstruction in the early Nineteenth century, when it was the property of Girolamo Egidio di Velo; at that time the vast "Hall of Apollo" was rearranged according to the neoclassic fashion. It was further modified in 1934 when it became the property of the Anselmi family, and once again when it was bought by Luigi Milan Massari. Purchased by the Banca Cattolica del Veneto, merged with the Ambroveneto and then associated with Banca Intesa, it has been subject of a radical and definitive restoration project aimed at adapting the interiors to a museum function. Along the halls on the main floor, where we find Baroque frescos by Alberti and Dorigny and statues by the Marinali brothers, the exhibition of the most famous part of the collection continues; it is a matter of the "Longhi Group" formerly held by the Corner-Spinelli museum in Venice. The second floor houses an exhibition of about 130 Russian icons chosen from the 500 comprising the rich collection of Banca Intesa.

*Palazzo Leoni-Montanari, now Banca Cattolica del Veneto*

Some of the most beautiful comprise the "Royal gates" (Moscow, late Sixteenth century), "the majesty of Christ" (Russian, Sixteenth century) and "The Archangels Michael and Gabriel" (Sixteenth century). As part of the cultural initiatives, masterpieces belonging to the public heritage are "Returned" after restoration every year.

Leaving the Palazzo we go back to visit the Tempio di Santa Corona, one of the town's most beautiful churches, which also holds a great number of works of art.

The church was begun in 1261, and was to have held the relics of Santa Spina, given to Bishop Bartolomeo da Breganze by King Louis IX of France. The facade, although restored, reserves its original appearance. The brickwork, doorway and side windows were all modified between 1872 and 1874.

The interior of the church has also undergone changes and extensions. The walls, originally frescoed were whitewashed during the Plague of 1630. The chapels were mainly built by the local nobility, and the most ornate, the last on the left, contains the Baptism of Jesus by Giovanni Bellini, and is one of his best works. In the fourth chapel on the right we find the "Adorazione dei Magi" by Paolo Veronese (1573). The Porto chapel holds the tomb of Luigi da Porto, auther of the novel "Giulietta e Romeo", and is the last work of Bartolomeo Montanga. The magnificent Rosario chapel (early 1600's) has marble decorations and paintings by Maganza and his school.

The altar, by Antonio Corberelli and his son Domenico is richly inlaid with mother of pearl, coral, lapislazuli, and jasper, in black stone. Behind are the ornate choirstalls with representations of a town which could be Vicenza in the 15th C.

At the bottom of the stairs leading from the presbitery we find a red marble urn containing the remains of count Palmiero Sesso, who founded the choir. From here we go down into the crypt, which has a number of statues and paintings.

Going back up into the church we find the Capella della Sacra Spina on the left of the Presbytery, and in the chapel a beautiful Gothic reliquary made in the 14th C. by Vicenza goldsmiths.

To the left a small door goes through to the antisacristy and the new Capitol, a huge room with aletenate, statues and tombs. Going back into the antisacristy we continue into the sacresty which contains among other valuable works the relics of S. Vincenzo. It is worth going out into the garden to admire the view of the Tempio and its beautiful belltower.

The old convent, located to the left of the Church, was destroyed during the war; its essential parts have been built as part of an extensive restoration project which has provided a venue for the archaeological and natural museum. Monastery of S. Corona in Contrà S. Corona (visits from Tuesday to Sunday). Collections: naturalistic section, installed on the ground floor of the western side of the

*Tempio di Santa Corona*

smaller monastery, where the naturalistic aspects of the Berici hills are shown through a description and exhibition of materials organised by environments. The exhibition itinerary commences with a general description of the hill environment, offering a synthetic scenario of the surface morphology of the karst area, the viability, the hydrography and the climate. The geological hall features lithological and palaeontologic finds illustrating the stratigraphic sequences composing the Berici. An ample documentation on the aquatic flora and fauna of the Fimon lake, and an archaeological section is presented on the first floor of the western wing of the monastery, dating from the Fifteenth century; and above all on the ground floor of the two monasteries, where finds from various locations of the Vicenza area are

41

exhibited, presented in chronological sequences.

The ancient convent to the left of the church is now being converted into a museum of archeology and nature.

Leaving the church we go down Corso Palladio towards Piazza Matteotti. Under the arch on the left is the tall narrow Casa Cogollo said to have been built by Palladio between 1560 and 1570. Reaching the square on our left we find the Castello dei Carraresi, held by various occupiers through the ages. The building was restored in 1930. Passing through the archway and the door to the north we come into the Odeo rooms, built by Scamozzi in 1582 and decorated by Maffei in 1635. To the left is a way through to the Teatro Olimpico, built between 1580

The "Territorio"

Palazzo Chiericati: now the Civic Museum

*Entrance to the Olympic Theatre garden*

and 1584 with funds from the Accademia Olimpica.
One's eye is immediately caught by the stage, at the centre
of which is a large arch capped by the emblem of the town.
The main body of the stage represents a square, whilst behind
are the five streets of Tebe, created by Scamozzi, who went
beyond Palladio's original intentions. From the stage we may
admire the rest of the theatre to which Palladio gave such a
sense of space.

   Leaving the theatre via the courtyard we come into Piazza
Matteotti, once completely surrounded by water, and which
has housed the Civic Museum in Palazzo Chiericati since 1855.
The building was commissioned by Girolamo Chiericati and

*Inside the Olympic Theatre. The set*

*Inside the Olympic Theatre. The seating and stage* (Foto Marton) gentilmente concessa dalla A.P.T. di Vicenza

# ITINERARY N. 3
## On foot. Time required: 2 hours

*Focal Points:*

1) Le Barche in Contrà Barche and Vicolo Cieco Retrone
2) Ponte S. Michele
3) Oratorio di S. Nicola - Piazzetta S. Nicola
4) Palazzo Valle - Contrà Busa San Michele
5) Palazzo Gualdo - Piazza Gualdi
6) Palazzo Porto Scaroni (teatro Berga) in front of Porton del Luzzo
7) Porton del Luzzo
8) Oratorio di S. Chiara in Contrà S. Chiara
9) Chiesa di S. Caterina in Contrà S. Caterina
10) Oratorio delle Zitelle in Contrà S. Caterina
11) Casa Pigafetta in Contrà Pigafetta
12) I Proti in Contrà Proti
13) Palazzi Arnaldi in Contrà Pasini
14) Chiesa delle Grazie in Piazzetta delle Grazie

## The Route:

Piazza Matteotti - Via Jacopo Cabianca - Le Barche - Vicolo Cieco Retrone - Contrà Piancoli - Ponte S. Michele - Piazzetta S. Nicola - Contrà Busa S. Michele - Via della Fossetta - Piazzetta Gualdi - Porton del Luzzo - Contrà San Tommaso - Contrà Santa Chiara - Contrà Santa Caterina - Contrà San Silvestro - Piazza San Giuseppe - Ponte Furo-Viale Eretenio.

Leaving Palazzo Chiericati we begin by going right towards Contrà Jacopo Cabianca. Here, beyond a small garden, is Palazzo Trento-Valmarana, built by Muttoni in 1718. It was

## *ITINERARY N. 3: from Piazza Matteotti to Piazza Castello*

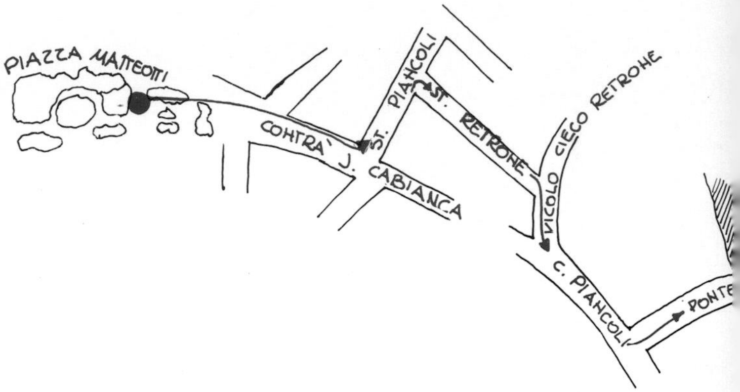


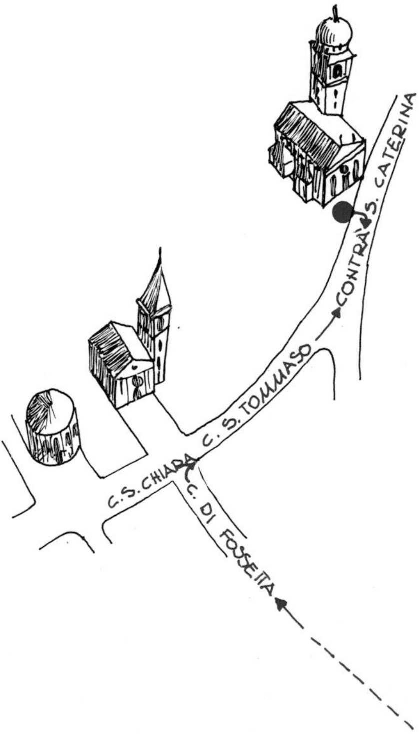

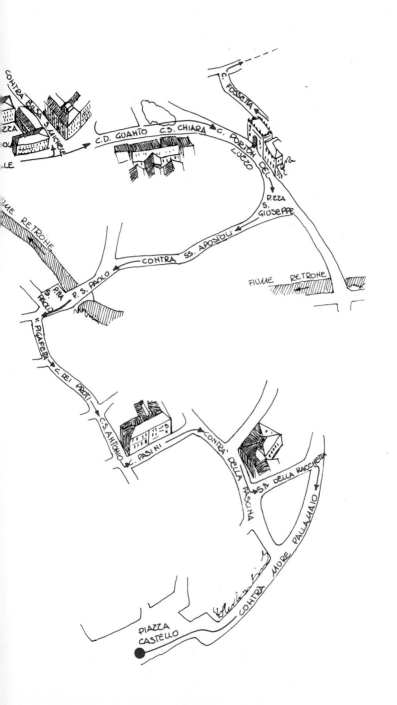

CONTRA PONTA SALICIERE

PZZA

QL

LE

C.D. GUANTO   C.S. CHIARA   C. PORTON DEL

LUZO

C. FOSSETTA

P.ZZA
S. GIUSEPPE

FIUME RETRONE

CONTRA SS. APOSTOLI

FIUME    RETRONE

P. S. PAOLO

P.TA
S.
PAOLO

V. PIGAFETTA

C. DEI PROTI

C.S. ANTONIO

C. PASINI

CONTRÀ DELLA RASCHA

S.A DELLA RACCHETTA

CONTRÀ MURE PALLAMAIO

PIAZZA
CASTELLO

49

badly damaged by bombing and fire in March 1945, when the stairs and frescoes were destroyed.

Continuing along Contrà Cabianca we go left into the Quartiere delle Barche, once the port on the river Retrone. Here we find a variety of buildings which were allowed to deteriorate until 1980 when a general restoration took place. Of particular note is the Ospedale di S. Valentino on Vicolo Cieco Retrone, which presents us with Gothic, Renaissance and Baroque in the one building.

Continuing along Contrà Piancoli we see Palazzo Nievo on the right and a number of interesting buildings on the left. We then come to Ponte S. Michele, the bridge built at the meeting point of the Retrone and Bacchiglione to a design by Tomaso and Francesco Contini, who also worked on the Rialto bridge in Venice. Built between 1621 and 1623 it is composed of a single arch. Over the bridge on the left is the oratorium S. Nicola da Tolentino, built in 1505, renovated between 1617 and 1633 and restored in 1946. On the left after the oratorium is

*View of Ponte Romano and the "Barche"*

*Ponte S. Michele*

Palazzo Valle, built in the 1600's and recently completely restored. Continuing along Contrà del Pozzetto we reach Piazzola Gualdi, named after the original owners of the two buildings dominating it. The first has an ashlar base, and the second, Palazzo 'Vecchio' was bought by Francesco Gualdo in 1499. Inside is an impressive square room where Emperor Charles V stayed when passing through Vicenza.

Carrying on towards Porton del Luzzo we come to Palazzo Pigafetta Porto (1700) under which can still be seen the Roman theatre of Berga (200 A.D.). The theatre took up the whole area between Piazzetta Gualdi, Piazza S. Giuseppe and Contrà SS. Apostoli.

The first excavations, in the last century, found signs of the main elements of the theatre, and in 1976 the Vicenza Chamber of Commerce funded research which confirmed the existence of a large theatre.

Opposite is Porton del Luzzo which connected Borgo Berga with the ancient town centre. Today Torre del Luzzo has been modified and spoilt by the addition of extra windows. Beyond the gateway, going along Contrà S. Tomaso towards Contrà S. Chiara we come to the Oratorio di S. Chiara or S. Bernardino, built in 1451 by Domenico di Giovanni from Venice.

Above the doorway is S. Bernardino, and moving inside we find the upper structure held up by eight red marble columns, octagonal at the base and round at the top.

Leaving the church we continue along Contrà S. Chiara, past the impressive Palazzo Pojana, now Palazzo Matteazzi, and then along Contrà S. Caterina, with the 17th C. church of S. Caterina on our left. This church, by Pizzocaro contains paintings which make up a virtual anthology of Veneto painting from the first half on the 16th C., as well as the inlaid

*Palazzo Valle*

*Palazzo Garzadori Braga*

marble tomb of Giovanni Maria Bertoli, founder of the Civic Library.

Opposite this church is the Oratorio delle Zitelle, built in 1647 by Antonio Pizzocaro. Inside are three altars with paintings by Maffei and Carponi. Next to S. Caterina is the ancient Ognissanti convent, which has passed through many hands and is now being restored after falling into a state of very bad repair.

Going along Via Generale Chinotto towards Contrà S. Silvestro we come to the church of S. Silvestro, which has also had a difficult past, being built around 1650 and after passing from one religious group to another being occupied by French soldiers in 1798. After 1810 the whole convent became a barracks and the church was closed. In 1866 the barracks were named after General Durango and were occupied by Alpine troops. Following the second World War the buildings were abandoned, with the church eventually being saved by restoration begun in 1951.

Going back down Contrà S. Silvestro past Porton del Luzzo we come to Piazzetta S. Giuseppe and then Ponte Furo which dates back to the 1200's, being widened in 1869. There is a picturesque view of the town from the bridge.

From here we continue along the wide Viale Eretenio, which is dominated by one of the early works of Palladio, Palazzo Civeno Trissino. Going back into Piazzetta S. Giuseppe we go along Contrà SS. Apostoli, which is full of small Gothic buildings.

*Casa Pigafetta*

*I Proti*

We now walk along Contrà S. Paolo and crossing the bridge over the Retrone, built by Della Veccha in 1875 we continue our walk along Contrà Pigafetta, coming to Casa Pigafetta built in 1481 (the date is on the side of the doorway). This beautiful building combines Renaissance and Late-Gothic styles and is unique in the whole of Veneto.

Continuing along Contrà Proti where we find the Ospizio dei Proti on our left. The building was begun in 1412 under instructions from Giampietro Proti who wanted to set up a hospice for members of the local nobility who had fallen on hard times. It was totally rebuilt by Palladio in 1658. The courtyard has four floors of enclosed terraces and has been recently restored.

We move on along Contrà S. Antonio with the medioeval Loschi towers on one right, and then go down Via Pasini, where we find the Late-Gothic and 15th C. Palazzetti Arnaldi.

Continuing down Contrà Fascina and Via delle Grazie we have an excellent view of the Chiesa delle Grazie, built in 1494, demolished in 1580, rebuilt in 1595 and restored only recent-

*Chiesa delle Grazie*

ly. It is believed to be the combined work of Antonio Pizzocaro and the Albanese family.

We now head towards Piazza Castello, going down Via della Racchetta (view of Palazzo Anti Veronese by Calderari), and Contrà Pallamaio, following the old town walls.

*Oratorio S. Chiara*

*Porton del Luzzo*

*The two "palazzi Arnaldi"*

## ITINERARY N. 4 (Bus no. 4 for S. Agostino)
## On foot. Time required: 3 1/2 hours

*Focal Points:*

1) Basilica di S. Felice in Corso S. Felice
2) Badia di S. Agostino
3) La Rocchetta
4) Chiesa S. Maria Nova in Contrà S. Maria Nova
5) Chiesa di S. Rocco in Piazzetta S. Rocco
6) Chiesa dei Carmini in Piazzetta dei Carmini
7) Palazzo Volpe-Gallo-Zaccaria. The "Vigna" Foundation
8) Chiesa di S. Croce
9) Porta S. Croce

## The Route:

From Piazzale De Gasperi - Corso S. Felice - Viale Verona - Via D'Annunzio - Passerella - Viale Sant'Agostino (bus) - Viale Verona - Corso S. Felice - Piazzale Giusti - Via Mure - Porta Nuova - Via Bonollo - Viale Mazzini (brietly) - return via Contrà Mure S. Rocco - Contrà S. Maria Nova - Piazzetta S. Rocco - Contrà Mure S. Rocco - Contrà Mure Corpus Domini - Via Busato - Corso Fogazzaro - Piazzetta dei Carmini - Contrà Porta S. Croce.

From Porta Castello to Porta S. Croce

We start from Piazzale De Gasperi, and go along Corso S. Felice past the Giardino Salvi. Borgo di S. Felice became part of the town itself only in the 1800's. The ancient origins of the area are pointed to by two churches, both now deconsacrated, the 17th C. S. Bovo and the 16th C. Chiesetta di S. Valentino. Crossing Viale Miolano and going past a number of buildings from the 1800's and early 1900's we come to a courtyard on our left, inside which we find the ancient buildings

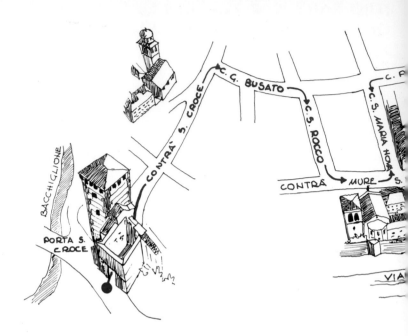

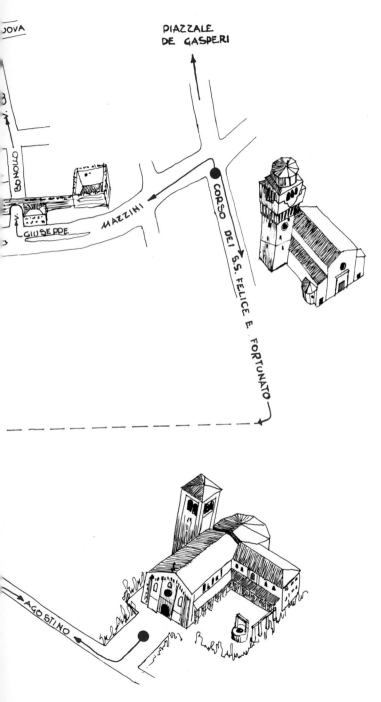

which comprise the Basilica dei SS. Felice e Fortunato, one of the most important examples of Paleo-Christian art in Northern Italy. It was originally built around 300, on a pagan burial ground, to hold the relics of the two Saints Vicenza Felice and Fortunato, who had been martyred around 303. Originally rectangular, the church was doubled in size and divided into 3 naves around the end of the last century. The Martirion was built in the 5th C. to hold the remains of other local martyrs. In 899 the Basilica was destroyed by the Hungarians, and only the Martirion and a part of the outside wall left standing. It was rebuilt in the 10th C., and was handed over to the Benedictine monks in 963. It was built on a similar plan shape, with the exception of the apse, which was semicircular, rather than rectangular. A new baptistry was built between the church and the Martirion, and by the site of the old one the bell tower was erected.

In 1117 an earthquake struck, causing structural damage, and during the restoration work the crypt was enlarged, as was

*Basilica SS. Felice and Fortunato*

*Abbey of S. Agostino*

*Abbey of S. Agostino: "Polittico" by Battista da Vicenza*

*Chiesa di S. Rocco*

the "Confessio" which holds the remains of Felice and Fortunato in a Greek marble urn. The upper part of the bell tower also dates from this period.

Baroque marble and stucco was added to the interior of the church at the end of the 17th C., and the original walls were uncovered only after work carried out following the second world war. Inside the Basilica we find the beautiful apse with frescoes by Carpioni, the 4th C Paleo-Christian mosaic floor, a statue of the Virgin Mary and a Gothic tabernacle by Antonion da Venezia. The garden also contains many very old pieces of masonry and sculpture, including a 4th C. sarcophagus lid. Leaving the garden we go along Viale Verona towards Via D'Annunzio, over the railway to the Ferrovieri (no. 4 bus-stop).

From have we reach the Badia di S. Agostino, near the Retrone. From 1188 to 1236 the chapel was given over to a lay organization, after which it passed into the hands of the friars of S. Bartolomeo. The friars found themselves in financial difficulties towards 1288, but it was not until 1319 that other friars were permitted to join them and restore the church. The church is in line with the style of the times, and the inside is a single large room with walls which were once all frescoed, as shown by those fragments remaining.

The presbytery is dominated by the polyptych on the altar commissioned from Battista de Vicenza, by Ludovico Chiericati in 1404, to celebrate the "dedication" of Vicenza to Venice. The whole ceiling of the Presbytery is frescoed. Leaving the church we can see, on the right, a rebuilt part of the Cloister and convent. The bell-tower tooks a little squat as it has no top.

We get the bus back to Viale Verona and then go down Corso S. Felice to Piazzale Giusti, the site, until 1030, of the

*Palazzo Volpe Gallo now Fondazione la Vigna*

medioeval Porta Nuova. We go down Contrà della Rocchetta, following the line of the medioeval city wall to the end of
the street where we find the fortified Rocchetta (ring the bell
of the "deposito comunale" to visit it). The fort was built in
1365 between the piece of wall coming from S. Felice and that
coming from S. Croce. This long piece of wall may be admired
right along Viale Mazzini as far as Porta S. Croce.

La Rocchetta was a real castle, with towers on each corner,
drawbridges, and a moat fed by the Seriola.

Carrying on towards Via del Quartiere we pass Palazzo
Schiavetto built by Calderari for the Bonin family, and going
along Via Mure Porta Nuova we come to Contrà S. Maria Nova
with the church of the same name, designed by Andrea Palladio, on the left. The church has a good collection of paintings
by late 16th C. Vicenza artists, and the key to see them may
be requested from the Parrocchia dei Carmini. The walk con-

*Porta S. Croce. Inside the walls*

tinues to Contrada Mure di S. Rocco, arriving at a small square dominated by the elegant facade of the recently restored Chiesa di S. Rocco.

Saint Rocco is known as the protector against the epidemics which were common between 1300 and 1600.

The church was built in 1485 under instructions from the town Council, who intended to give it over to a religious order, and thus built a monastery nearby which, after a few years, was enlarged. The council chose the lay canons of S. Giorgio in Alga, who stayed until they were replaced by the Carmelite monks in 1670. In 1806, as a result of a secularization following the French Revolution it become a hospice, which in 1886 became a hospice for abandoned children. Finally in 1958 it became the Provincial Institute for Child Welfare, which it remains.

Since 1975, the old part of S. Rocco, next to the church, has held the Institute of Social and Religious History. Built in

1530 it has been restored twice, between 1922 and 1925, and in 1987. The interior is by Lorenzo da Bologna and the altars are richly decorated by famous local artists, Zelotti and Maganza. The walls are "crustae" frescoed and the floor has a geometrical pattern in multi-coloured marble. The most interesting parts from an architectural point of view however are the convent and the cloisters, built between 1494 and 1580 by Lorenzo da Bologna.

Coming out of the church we continue along Contrada Mure S. Rocco as far as Contrà Mure Corpus Domini, where we turn right, going along Via Busato to Corso Fogazzaro. In the Piazzetta dei Carmini is the church of S. Maria del Carmine, which dates back to 1373, but was greatly altered in 1862 in a neo-Gothic style. The inside is a splendid example of Renaissance art, with the chapels, side altars and doors dating back to the late 1400's. We can also admire paintings by the De Pieri, Carpioni, Bassano and Montagna.

*Torrioncino Veneziano in Viale d'Alviano*

*Torrioncino Veneziano in Viale d'Alviano. Exterior view*

Leaving by the side door we go along Contrà Porto S. Croce, dominated on the left by a neoclassical building from 1833 by Tommaso Becega. This is the seat of the "Fondazione La Vigna" donated, together with the building, by the proprieter, who collected antique and modern books on agriculture from all over the world. The collection may be viewed during office hours.

The walk ends at Porta S. Croce, a few metres from which is the Chiesa S. Croce, an ancient building enlarged in the 1700's, with an atrium by Muttoni. Until 1179 the church had a pilgrims' hospital attached to it.

Porta S. Croce which finishes our walk is one of the best preserved details of the city wall. We can still see the housings for the draw-bridges, if we look carefully.

Not far from the Porta along the way which in Roman times went from Viale Brotton to the centre of the town is the archeological site discovered in 1979, which contains supporting pillars from the Roman aqueduct which came from Motta di Costabissara, where there was plenty of water with a constant flow, temperature and chemical content.

## ITINERARY N. 5
## On foot. Time required: 2 hours

*Focal Points:*

1) Chiesa di S. Marco in Contrà S. Marco
2) Parco Querini. Viale Bacchiglione
3) Chiesa dell'Araceli. Piazza Araceli
4) Porta S. Lucia
5) Palazzo Magrè Angaran. Piazza XX Settembre
6) Ponte degli Angeli
7) Corte dei Roda. Contrà S. Andrea
8) Chiesa di S. Pietro. Piazzetta S. Pietro
9) Oratorio dei Boccalotti
10) S. Domenico in Contrà S. Domenico

## The Route:

Contrà Porta S. Croce - Ponte Nuovo - Contrà della Misercordia - Contrà S. Marco - Contrà Chioare - Viale Bacchiglione - Piazza Araceli - Porta S. Lucia - Contrà S. Lucia - Piazza XX Settembre - Contrà S. Pietro - Vicolo S. Andrea - Contrà S. Domenico - Ponte degli Angeli - Piazza Matteotti.

From Porta S. Croce we go back taking the road on the left which takes us slightly uphill to the Ponte Nuovo, an iron bridge over the Bacchiglione, built in 1882. The banks of this river were once lined by washer-women who did the washing for virtually the whole town. Carrying on along Via della Misericordia past the ancient church of S. Maria Maddalena (now restored and transformed into a wonderful architect's studio) further on the left we come to the Ospizio della Misericordia founded by S. Girolamo Ermigliani in the 1550s. It was recently restored following virtual collapse. Built in 1594 it may be the work of Scamozzi but is more probably by Pizzocaro. We go out into Contra S. Marco where we find the facade of the Chie-

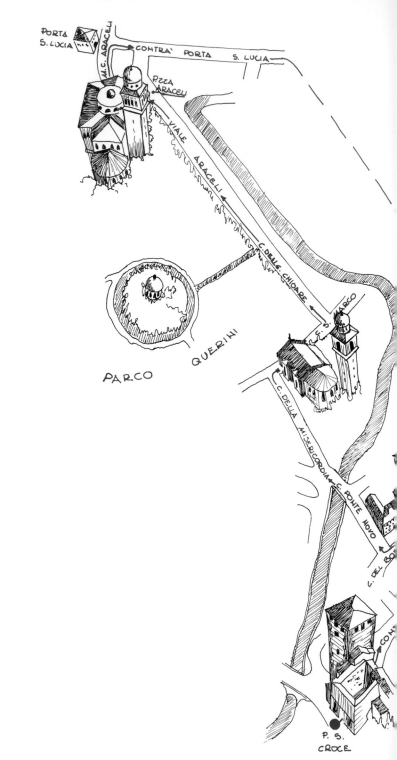

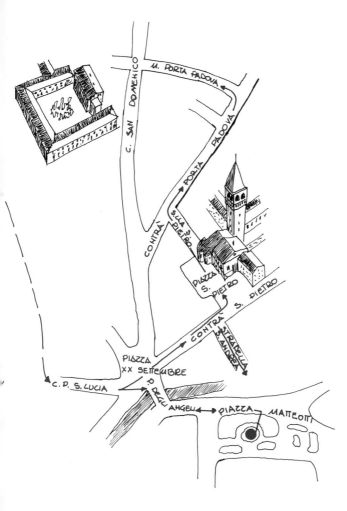

*Chiesa di S. Marco*

sa di S. Marco, commonly called Chiesa degli Scalzi. It was built on the site of the ancient oratorium of S. Girolamo and a church attached to the convent of the Jesuits closed by Napoleon. The bell-tower is the only remaining part of the original buildings. The front of the church the last example of Baroque architecture in Vicenza is by Corbellini. The inside of the church is spacious with high side chapels. Among the various paintings is a rare work by the young Batista Maganza: "S. Girolamo Penitente".

Along Contra S. Marco a series of noble buildings give the road a distinguished air: Palazzo Piovene is next to Palazzetto Angaran Vaccari by Palladio and on the left is Palazzo Franceschini built in 1770 by Scamozzi. At the end of Contra S. Marco turning left passing between tall buildings where once stood two mills we continue along Via Chioare. Here we stop for a moment: on the right is the Ponte Pusterla which linked the old town centre with Borgo Pusterla beyond the city walls.

This area was marshy and easily flooded, being close to what was left of the old lake "Lacus Pausterlae". All this water encouraged the presence of water and woollen mills as well as a printers. Here the Bacchiglione was fed by canals which helped to move the water wheels. On the left of the ruins is the Parco Querini, a green oasis in the heart of the city. A municipal park since after the war it was originally part of the Palazzo Capra-Querini, and contains 18th C. statues by such famous sculptors as Marinali, Gai and Putti. The Ionic temple (1820) is by Antonio Piovene.

Just beyond the exit, Viale Bacchiglione opens out into a square containing the Chiesa di S. Maria in Araceli. There has been a church on this site since at least 1214. In 1675 the church was demolished to make way for a larger building consecrated in 1743. When the French army arrived in 1797 the nuns had to leave the church, coming back in 1799. In 1810

*Parco Querini*

*Chiesa di Araceli*

*Porta S. Lucia*

when the religious orders were suppressed the property of the nuns was handed over to Count Antonio Capra who demolished the convent. Since 1813 the church has been a parish church and since 1978 has been undergoing restoration.

Leaving the church we go along Contrà Mura Aroceli until we reach Porta S. Lucia built by the Scaligeri in 1369 to replace a wooden drawbridge: Above the archway is a bas-relief of the Lion of S. Marco. From Porta S. Lucia we carry on towards the old town centre along Contrada S. Lucia until we reach Piazza XX Settembre. This is a typical Vicenza street of small houses and larger middle class homes dating back to the 16th C.

At the end of the contrada on the right is Palazzo Magre Angaran. The building has arches running round it and the facade facing Contrada S. Lucia has a beautiful quadrifora window. Constant flooding of the Bacchiglione caused the steady sinking of the main door which was demolished and rebuilt at the new street level in the 1930's. We continue, crossing Ponte degli Angeli which was originally a Roman bridge over the Astico, until the Astico was diverted to be replaced by the Bacchiglione.

The bridge has undergone a number of transformations down the ages including restoration by Palladio in 1550-1560 following flooding. In 1882 the decision was taken to replace the old foundations with iron piers. From Piazza XX Settembre we carry on along Contrada S. Pietro turning right into Contra S. Andrea to reach the Corte dei Roda. The buildings running along the left back of the Bacchiglione were designed by Scamozzi. The whole area was recently rescued from a state of disrepair which has saved, in part, the original structure.

*Palazzo Angaran*

Leaving by Via Nazario Sauro to Contrada di S. Pietro we reach Piazza S. Pietro overlooked by the 15th C. church of the same name. The church holds paintings by Maganza, Zelotti and Maffei. On the right of the door a memorial stone in gothic

*Palazzo Regaù*

*Corte dei Roda*

*Chiesa di S. Pietro*

*Oratorio dei Boccalotti*

writing recalls the burial of Elica the founder of the convent of S. Pietro in 827 A.D. On the right of the church is the convent, home of the Benedictine monks until the arrival of Napoleon in 1810. In the church yard is the simple Oratorio dei Boccalotti with a beautiful terracotta decoration above the door.

Leaving the square we go along Contrada S. Pietro and turn right into contra di Porta Padova. Of particular note here is the 15th C. Palazzo Regain, one of the best Gothic buildings in Vicenza.

We continue along Contra S. Domenico until we reach the church of the same name dating back to the 13th C. when the Domenican monks established themselves in Vicenza. The facade of the church, whilst showing signs of the restoration carried out last century actually dates back to the 1300's. Inside is the original clay floor whilst the choir stalls date back to the 16th C. The cloisters, among the biggest in Vicenza, were rebuilt in 1483. Also worth seeing is the refectory with

*S. Domenico: "Adorazione dei Magi" by Alesandro Maganza*

its 15th C. vaulted ceiling. Leaving the church we make our
way back towards Ponte degli Angeli and Piazza Matteotti.

# ITINERARY N. 6
## From Piazza Matteotti to Porta Castello or the station
## On foot. Time required: 3 ¹/₂ hours

*Focal Points:*

1) Arco delle Scalette - Piazzale Fraccon
2) Villa Valmarana ai Nani - Piazzetta S. Bastiano
3) Villa Capra "La Rotonda" - Strada Valmarana
4) Basilica di Monte Berico
5) Piazzale della Vittoria
6) Villa Guiccioli and park (Risorgimento Museum) Viale X Giugno
7) Portici
8) Chiesetta di S. Giorgio in Viale Fusinato

## The Route:

Piazza Matteotti - Viale Giuriolo - Viale Margherita - Piazzale Fraccon - Le Scalette - Piazzale D'Azeglio - Stradella S. Bastiano - Stradella Valmarana - Viale X Giugno - Piazzale della Vittoria - Viale X Giugno (out and back) - I Portici - Piazzale S. Libera - Viale Fusinato (out and back) - Porta Lupia - Viale Dalmazia - Piazzale De Gasperi.

From Piazza Matteotti to Piazza Castello

We leave Piazza Matteotti and go along Viale Giuriola with the Retrone on our right and the Bacchiglione on our left. Going over the crossroads we carry on along Viale Margherita. At the end of the road is the Arco degli Scalette built by Capitano Giacomo Bragadin of the Venetian Republic in honour of the Virgin Mary of Monte Berico. The arch was designed by Palladio and the statues are by the Albanese. Behind the arch is the stairway of 192 steps. At the top of these stairs we come onto Via D'Azeglio which opens out into an oval square marked

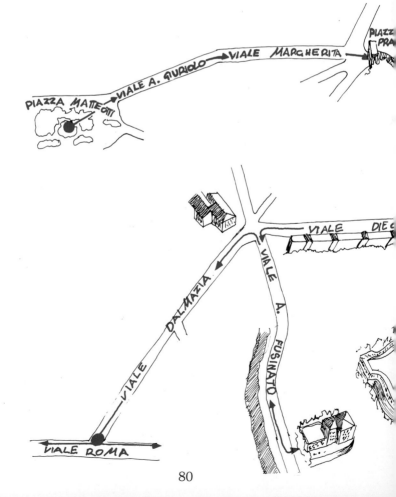

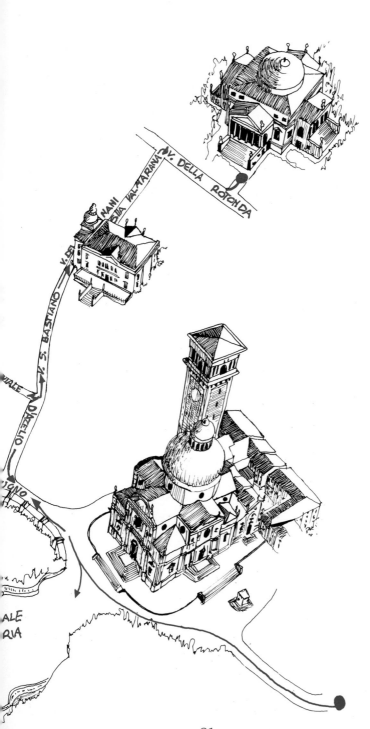

V. DELLA ROTONDA

V. SIA VALMARANA

NANI

V. B.

V. S. BASTIANO

IALE

D'ARELIO

GNO

ALE

RIA

by four pyramids. We go along Stradella di San Bastiano coming to the crossing with Stradella Gianbattista Tiepolo which goes up to Borgo Berga and from where start the grounds of Villa Valmarana which has a series of small grotesque statues along the outside wall. This villa, as was the fashion in the 1700's, is made up of a number of buildings with different functions. The main building in the centre of the garden was designed by Muttoni in 1669. The villa itself belonged to Gian Maria Bertolo who founded the civic library. Inside, the ground floor rooms are completely frescoed by Gianbattista Tiepolo with a little help from his son Giandomenico and date from 1757.

The ground floor rooms contain a wealth of paintings which merit a visit in themselves.

Leaving the villa and crossing the garden we enter the "Foresteria" where a large entrance hall links all the other rooms. Here again there are a large number of works of art by father

*Arco delle Scalette*

*Villa Valmarana "Ai Nani"*

and son Tiepolo. Once our visit is finished we go along the private road Valmarana which takes us to the "Rotonda", Palladio's masterpiece built between 1550 and 1552 as a retirement home for Canon Paolo Almerico.

The building consists of a cubic construction with the four corners perfectly aligned with the cardinal points to make the maximum effect of light and shade on the walls. Each of the four facades has a pronaos with six ionic columns and staircase. The name Rotonda comes from the plan shape of the building, a circle inside a square. The dome is by Vincenzo Scamozzi who changed Palladio's plans, lowering it.

The villa is divided into three floors. The first, at entry level, is the most highly decorated. The ground floor contained kitchens, laundry and servants quarters and is not highly decorated but of great architectural beauty. The upper floor, originally one large room, was used as a store room and was defined by Palladio as "a walking place" around the dome. Spiral staircases lead from one floor to another.

The central ceiling paintings date from around the end of the 16th C. and are by Alessandro Maganza and his son Giambattista.

*Villa Capra "La Rotonda". Aerial view*

The frescoes by Dorigny in the main central room, the corridors and on the plasterwork are from a more recent modernizing of the villa.

Going back down Stradella Valmarana, returning to Stradella S. Bastiano, we come to Viale X Giugno which leads up to the Basilica di Monte Berico. According to a popular belief the first church dedicated to the Madonna of Monte Berico was built on the site where the Virgin Mary appeared to Vincenza Pasini in 1426 and 1428 while the inhabitants of the town were dying of the plague. The Madonna promised that it the people of Vicenza built a church on the top of the hill she would rid them of the plague. The church was built in three months. In 1476 it was extended by Lorenzo da Bologna. The building, including a partially finished addition by Palladio was knocked down and in 1688 the task of building a new Basilica was given to Carlo Borella. He designed a building in the shape of a Greek cross which isolated the simple Gothic church which over the years had been altered both inside and out.

*Villa Capra "La Rotonda". The central room, seen from the north*

*Villa Capra "La Rotonda". Detail of the ceiling in the side room to the east*

*Bird's eye's view of the Sanctuary of Monte Berico and Piazzale della Vittoria*
(Foto Colorfoto) gentilmente concessa dalla A.P.T. di Vicenza

*The Santuario di Monte Berico with the "Portici"*

*Monte Berico. Interior*

88

*Santuario di Monte Berico*

The new Basilica was finished in 1703, and has three identical facades, richly decorated by Orazio Marinali. It is built on a terrace which was extended in 1817, by Verda, who also added three sets of steps, one in front of each facade. Inside, behind the main altar we find the statue of the Madonna della Misericordia from 1444, in coloured marble, thought to be by Antonio da Venezia. To the right of the altar is the famous fresco of the "Pietà" by Montagna.

Leaving the Basilica to the left of the altar we come into the Convento dei Padri Serviti, in the refectory of which we find the magnificent "Cena di S. Gregorio Magno" by Paolo Veronese (1572). The painting was stolen by French soldiers, but was fortunately recovered and brought back to the church, having being cut up into thirty-two pieces by Austrian mercenaries during the battle of June 10th 1848. Thanks to Francesco Giuseppe d'Austria it was restored and placed where it is now found, in 1858.

Leaving the Receptory we move on to the Cloisters, where we find the original architecture remains intact. The well-head

*Santuario di Monte Berico: "La Pietà" by Bartolomeo Montagna*

was replaced in 1977, having been removed and placed in front of Villa Ambellicopoli-Giuccioli.

Leaving the building we find ourselves in Piazzale della Vittoria, thus named after the first World War. From here we have a wonderful view of the town, the Padana Plain and the Prealps. Going along Viale X Giugno, following the crest of the hill, we come to the Museo del Risorgimento e della Resistenza, on the Ambellicopoli hill. The villa was built in the late 1700's, for Marino Ambellicopoli. The second owner, the Marquis Giuccioli, added a small oratorium in 1855. The villa was the scene of stout defence during the battle for Vicenza in 1848, and thus when it became council property it was chosen as venue for the Museum of Renaissance and Resistance.

Now extensively restored the muse-um is well worth a visit.

*Santuario di Monte Berico:*
*"Incoronazione della Vergine con Santi"*
*(1606) by Palma il Giovane* ▶

Going back towards the Sanctuary we pass the "portici" built
by Muttoni in the second half of the 18th C., to replace the
fifteen small chapels built by Natele Bargie in 1614.

Each chapel refered to a mystery of the rosary, and Muttoni's "portici" have the fifteen mysteries shown in frescoes, one
every ten arches. The total length of the construction is 700
metres.

*Santuario di Monte Berico: Detail of "Cena di S. Gregorio Magno" (1572) by Paolo Veronese*

At the bottom we go along Viale Fusinato to the small church of S. Giorgio built in the 10th C. on slightly raised land to protect it from flooding. This simple church was an isolation hospital during the 1500's and the site of capital punishments during Austrian occupation. It became a parish church in 1963, following restoration.

Chiesa di S. Giorgio

Parco Villa Guiccioli, now "Museo del Risorgimento e della Resistenza"

The most interesting architectural feature is the polygonal apse. The restoration of the single outside walls was carried out using original Paleo-Christian materials, where possible.

Going back to Piazzale Santa Libera and Porta Lupia we continue along the once tree-lined Viale Dalmazia, which has now been partly replanted, and finally reach Piazzale De Gasperi and Porta Castello.

## Bibliographie

Barbieri F. e Cevese R., Vicenza e la sua Provincia (Guida breve). Vicenza 1950.

Barbieri F. Cevese R. Magagnato L., Guida di Vicenza. Eretemie editrice, Vicenza 1956.

Morsolin B., Le fonti della storia di Vicenza. Venezia 1881.

Mantese G., Memorie storiche della chiesa vicentina Vol. I, Vicenza 1952.

Cabianca I. Lampertico F., Vicenza e il suo territorio, Milano 1861.

Pullé G. Album di gemme architettoniche, Vicenza 1847.

De Mori G., Chiese e chiostri di Vicenza, Vicenza, 1928. Vicenza, città del Palladio, Vicenza 1931. Vicenza e la sua provincia, Vicenza, 1932.

Morsolin B., L'acquedotto romano e il teatro Berga di Vicenza, Venezia 1884.

Girardi M., La topografia di Vicenza Romana. Venezia 1923.

Lorenzon G., La Basilica dei SS. Felice e Fortunato, Quaderni n. 5 e una Appendice, Vicenza, 1934, 1948. La chiesa protocristiana di S. Silvestro. Giornale di Vicenza 20 novembre 1941.

Rumor G. S. Lorenzo nella storia e nell'arte, Vicenza, 1914.

Bortolan D., Santa Corona, Chiesa e convento dei Domenicani in Vicenza. Vicenza 1889.

## Photographs

G. Rossato, G. Pasqualotto, Studio V. Maino, P. Barbieri, Fototecnica, Archivio APT

---

**Visiting hours**

Villa La Rotonda
Every day except Monday, from 15th March to 15th October
Hours: 10 - 12
      15 - 18

Building open Wednesday

Villa Valmarana "Ai Nani"
Every day except Monday, from 15th March to 15th October
Hours: 10 - 12
      14,30 - 17,30

---